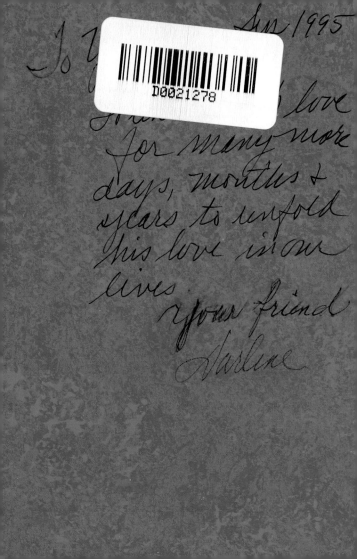

To Y____
Jun 1995

____ love
For many more
days, months &
years to unfold
this love in our
lives.

your friend

Darlene

Other mini books in this series:

Cat Quotations   Teddy Bear Quotations
Golf Quotations   Music Lover's Quotations
Horse Quotations   Book Lover's Quotations
Love Quotations   Garden Lover's Quotations
Happiness Quotations   Cricket Quotations

Published in the USA in 1992 by Exley Giftbooks
Published in Great Britain in 1992 by Exley Publications Ltd
Reprinted November 1992
Third and fourth printings 1993
Copyright © Helen Exley 1992
Series editor Helen Exley

ISBN 1-85015-317-5

A copy of the CIP data is available from the British Library on
request.

Designed by Pinpoint Design Company.
Pictures researched by Image Select.
Typeset by Delta, Watford.
Printed and bound in Hungary.

**Exley Publications Ltd, 16 Chalk Hill, Watford,
Herts WD1 4BN, United Kingdom.
Exley Giftbooks, 359 East Main Street, Suite 3D,
Mount Kisco, NY 10549, USA.**

Exley Publications is very grateful to the following individuals and
organizations for permission to reproduce their pictures: © Amand-Jean,
Edmond 'Two Ladies on a Chaise Longue: 30; Archiv Für Kunst; Christ
Beetles Ltd; Bonhams, London; Bradford City Art Gallery; Bridgeman Art
Library; Fine Art Society, London; © Lawson, Gillian 'Dancing on the
Water III: 40/41; Josef Mensing Gallery; David Messum Fine Paintings;
Musée D'Orsay, Paris; Musée Fabre, Montpellier; Royal Collection,
London; Scala; © Sharp, Dorothea 'Three Children Bathing': 10; Taylor
Gallery, London; Christopher Wood Gallery, London.

FRIENDSHIP QUOTATIONS

A COLLECTION OF
BEAUTIFUL PICTURES AND THE
BEST FRIENDSHIP QUOTES

– ◆ –

EDITED BY
HELEN EXLEY

EXLEY
MT. KISCO, NEW YORK • WATFORD, UK

NEVER NEEDING TO SAY

"Silences make the real conversations between friends. Not the saying but the never needing to say is what counts."

MARGARET LEE RUNBECK

— ◆ —

"For what do my friends stand? Not for the clever things they say: I do not remember them half an hour after they are spoken. It is always the unspoken, the unconscious, which is their reality to me."

MARK RUTHERFORD (1831-1913)

— ◆ —

"A friend hears the song in my heart and sings it to me when my memory fails."

from *"Pioneer Girls Leaders' Handbook"*

— ◆ —

"... that is the best - to laugh with someone because you both think the same thing is funny."

GLORIA VANDERBILT, b.1924

– ◆ –

"A joy shared is a joy doubled."

GOETHE (1749-1832)

– ◆ –

"Happiness seems made to be shared."

JEAN RACINE (1639-1699)

– ◆ –

"There's nothing worth the wear of winning, but laughter and the love of friends."

HILAIRE BELLOC (1870-1953)

– ◆ –

"Grief can take care of itself, but to get the full value of a joy you must have somebody to divide it with."

MARK TWAIN (1835-1910)

OATHS OF FRIENDSHIP

If you were riding in a coach
And I were wearing a *li*[1],
And one day we met in the road,
You would get down and bow.
If you were carrying a *teng*[2]
And I were riding on a horse,
And one day we met in the road
I would get down for you

[1] *peasant's straw hat*   [2] *hawker's umbrella*

I want to be your friend
For ever and ever without break or decay.
When the hills are all flat
And the rivers are all dry,
When it lightens and thunders in winter,
When it rains and snows in summer,
When Heaven and Earth mingle-
Not till then will I part from you.

CHINESE 1st CENTURY AD, tr. Arthur Waley

HOLD A TRUE FRIEND . . .

Hold a true friend with both hands.

NIGERIAN PROVERB

– ◆ –

"Treat your friends as you do your pictures,
and place them in their best light."

JENNIE JEROME CHURCHILL (1854-1921)

– ◆ –

"Do not keep the alabaster boxes of your
love and tenderness sealed up until your
friends are dead.
Fill their lives with sweetness. Speak
approving, cheering words while their ears
can hear them and while their hearts can be
thrilled by them."

HENRY WARD BEECHER (1813-1887)

– ◆ –

"Friendship, on the other hand, serves a great host of different purposes all at the same time. In whatever direction you turn, it still remains yours. No barrier can shut it out. It can never be untimely; it can never be in the way. We need friendship all the time, just as much as we need the proverbial prime necessities of life, fire and water."

CICERO (106-43 BC)

— ◆ —

Make new friends, but keep the old;
Those are silver, these are gold.
New-made friendships, like new wine,
Age will mellow and refine.
Friendships that have stood the test -
Time and change - are surely best.
Brow may wrinkle, hair grow gray;
Friendship never knows decay.
For 'mid old friends, tried and true,
Once more our youth renew.
But old friends, alas! may die;
New friends must their place supply.
Cherish friendship in your breast -
New is good, but old is best;
Make new friends, but keep the old;
Those are silver, these are gold.

JOSEPH PARRY

− ◆ −

"And a youth said, Speak to us of Friendship.
And he answered, saying:
Your friend is your needs answered.
He is your field which you sow with love and
reap with thanksgiving.
And he is your board and your fireside.
For you come to him and your hunger,
and you seek him for peace."

KAHLIL GIBRAN (1833-1931)

— ◆ —

"And all people live, not by reason of any care they have for themselves, but by the love for them that is in other people."

LEO TOLSTOY (1828-1910)

– ◆ –

THE LOSS OF A FRIEND

"How shall you speak of parting?
How shall the bands be loosened
That Friendship fastened round you?"

MADELINE MASON-MANHEIM, b.1908

— ♦ —

"I think there is, in friendship, an instant
recognition – a kind of loving. It needs just a
word, the touch of a hand – yet parting is
loss and the tiny ache of regret stays
with us always."

HELEN M. EXLEY

— ♦ —

"Odd how much it hurts when a friend moves
away - and leaves behind only silence."

PAM BROWN, b. 1928

— ♦ —

NOTHING MORE PRECIOUS

"Life is nothing without friendship."

CICERO (106-43 BC)

— ◆ —

"Life is to be fortified by many friendships.
To love, and to be loved, is the greatest
happiness of existence."

SYDNEY SMITH (1771-1845)

— ◆ —

"There's nothing more precious in this world
than the feeling of being wanted."

DIANA DORS (1931-1984)

— ◆ —

"Wherever you are it is your own friends who
make your world."

WILLIAM JAMES (1842-1910)

— ◆ —

LITTLE THINGS

"Friendships are glued together with
little kindnesses."

MERCIA TWEEDALE, b.1915

— ♦ —

"When a friend asks there is no tomorrow."

GEORGE HERBERT (1593-1633)

— ♦ —

"It's the friends you can call up at 4 a.m.
that matter."

MARLENE DIETRICH (1901-1992)

— ♦ —

"It is not so much our friends' help that helps
us as the confident knowledge that
they will help us."

EPICURUS (341-270 BC)

— ♦ —

FOR WHAT YOU ARE . . .

"When your friend speaks his mind you fear
not the 'nay' in your own mind, nor do you
withhold the 'ay.'
"And when he is silent your heart ceases not
to listen to his heart;
"For without words, in friendship, all
thoughts, all desires, all expectations
are born and shared, with joy that is
unacclaimed.
"When you part from your friend,
you grieve not;
"For that which you love most in him
may be clearer in his absence, as the
mountain to the climber is clearer from
the plain."

KAHLIL GIBRAN (1883-1931)

— ◆ —

"One is taught by experience to put a premium on those few people who can appreciate you for what you are. . ."

GAIL GODWIN, b.1937

– ◆ –

"Of what help is anyone who can only be approached with the right words?"

ELIZABETH BIBESCO (1897-1945)

– ◆ –

IN TRIUMPH AND DISASTER

". . . It is that my friends have made the story
of my life. In a thousand ways they have
turned my limitations into beautiful
privileges, and enabled me to walk serene and
happy in the shadow cast by my deprivation."

HELEN KELLER (1880-1968)

— ◆ —

"Friendship is not diminished by distance or time, by imprisonment or war, by suffering or silence. It is in these things that it roots most deeply."

PAM BROWN, b.1928

— ◆ —

"Friends, companions, lovers, are those who treat us in terms of our unlimited worth to ourselves. They are closest to us who best understand what life means to us, who feel for us as we feel for ourselves, who are bound to us in triumph and disaster, who break the spell of our loneliness."

HENRY ALONZO MYERS

— ◆ —

"What do we live for, if it is not to make life less difficult for each other?"

GEORGE ELIOT (MARY ANN EVANS) (1819-1880)

— ◆ —

Love is like the wild rose-briar;
Friendship like the holly-tree.
The holly is dark when the rose-briar blooms,
But which will bloom most constantly?

EMILY BRONTË (1818-1848)

— ♦ —

"Oh, the comfort, the inexpressible comfort, of feeling safe with a person; having neither to weigh thoughts nor measure words, but to pour them all out just as they are, chaff and grain together, knowing that a faithful hand will take and sift them, keep what is worth keeping, and then, with the breath of kindness, blow the rest away."

GEORGE ELIOT (MARY ANN EVANS) (1819-1880)

— ♦ —

"The truth in friendship is to me every bit as sacred as eternal marriage."

KATHERINE MANSFIELD (1888-1923)

"Trouble is a part of your life,
and if you don't share it,
you don't give the person who loves you
enough chance to love you enough."

DINAH SHORE, b.1917

– ◆ –

"If a friend of mine . . . gave a feast, and did
not invite me to it, I should not mind a bit . . .
But if . . . a friend of mine had a sorrow and
refused to allow me to share it, I should feel it
most bitterly. If he shut the doors of the house
of mourning against me, I would move back
again and again and beg to be admitted, so
that I might share in what I was entitled to
share. If he thought me unworthy, unfit to
weep with him, I should feel it as the most
terrible mode for which disgrace could be
inflicted on me . . . "

OSCAR WILDE (1854-1900)

FRIENDSHIP BELIEVES ALL THINGS

Friends are patient and kind,
they are not jealous or boastful,
they are not arrogant or rude.

Friends do not insist on having
their own way,
they are not irritable or resentful,
they do not rejoice at wrong,
but delight in what is right.

Friendship bears all things,
believes all things,
hopes all things,
endures all things.

Friendship
never ends.

Adapted from CORINTHIANS 1

— ◆ —

BLIND TO ALL FAULTS

"...to find a friend one must close one eye:
to keep him, two."

NORMAN DOUGLAS (1868-1952)

— ◆ —

"Every man should have a fair sized cemetery
in which to bury the faults of his friends."

HENRY BROOKS ADAMS (1838-1918)

— ◆ —

One who looks for a friend without faults
will have none.

HASIDIC SAYING

— ◆ —

"If the first law of friendship is that it has to
be cultivated, the second law is to be
indulgent when the first law has
been neglected."

VOLTAIRE (1694-1778)

— ◆ —

"You can grow old and saggy and baggy and slow, take to spectacles and dentures and develop a Widow's Hump.
But to your friend you are just as you were in the last year at school."

MARION C. GARRETTY, b. 1917

— ◆ —

"Ah, how good it feels!
The hand of an old friend."

HENRY WADSWORTH LONGFELLOW (1807-1882)

THE ARROW AND THE SONG

I shot an arrow into the air,
It fell to earth, I knew not where;
For, so swiftly it flew, the sight
Could not follow it in its flight.

I breathed a song into the air,
It fell to earth, I knew not where;
For who has sight so keen and strong,
That it can follow the flight of song?

Long, long afterward, in an oak
I found the arrow, still unbroke;
And the song, from beginning to end,
I found again in the heart of a friend.

HENRY WADSWORTH LONGFELLOW (1807-1882)

– ◆ –

"Remember the old saying, a friend in need is a damned nuisance."

PETER POOK, d.1979

— ◆ —

"A friend that isn't in need is a friend indeed."

KIN HUBBARD

— ◆ —

"He is a fine friend. He stabs you in the front."

LEONARD LOUIS LEVINSON

— ◆ —

"Whenever a friend succeeds, a little something in me dies."

GORE VIDAL, b.1925

— ◆ —

PUTTING UP WITH OUR FRIENDS

"How much easier to make pets of our
friends' weaknesses than to put up
with their strengths."

ELIZABETH BIBESCO (1897-1945)

– ◆ –

"There is nothing in the world I wouldn't do
for [Bob] Hope, and there is nothing he
wouldn't do for me.... We spend our lives
doing nothing for each other."

BING CROSBY (Harry Lillis) (1904-1977)

– ◆ –

"We are not greatly pleased by our friends
respecting our good qualities if they also
venture to perceive our faults."

VAUVENARGUES (1715-1747)

– ◆ –

FINDING A FRIEND

"Two may talk together under the same roof
for many years, yet never really meet; and two
others at first speech are old friends."

MARY CATHERWOOD (1847-1901)

— ◆ —

"Each friend represents a world in us, a world
possibly not born until they arrive, and it is
only by this meeting that a new world is born."

ANAÏS NIN (1903-1977)

— ◆ —

"To cement a new friendship, especially
between foreigners or persons of a different
social world, a spark with which both were
secretly charged must fly from person
to person, and cut across the accidents
of place and time."

GEORGE SANTAYANA (1863-1952)

— ◆ —

AT THEIR WORST

"Anyone can sympathize with the suffering of
a friend, but it requires a fine nature to
sympathize with a friend's success."

OSCAR WILDE (1856-1900)

— ◆ —

"But of all plagues, good Heaven,
thy wrath can send,
Save me, oh, save me, from the
candid friend."

GEORGE CANNING (1770-1827)

— ◆ —

"If we were all given by magic the power to
read each other's thoughts, I suppose the first
effect would be to dissolve all friendships."

BERTRAND RUSSELL (1872-1970)

— ◆ —

"There was nothing
wrong with her that a
vasectomy of the vocal
chords wouldn't fix."

LISA ALTHER, b.1944

— ♦ —

"Friendship will not
stand the strain of very
much good advice for
very long."

ROBERT LYND

— ♦ —

"Friendship is not
possible between two
women one of whom is
very well dressed."

LAURIE COLWIN

— ♦ —

TWINS IN SOUL

"There can be no friendship where there is no freedom. Friendship loves a free air, and will not be penned up in straight and narrow enclosures. It will speak freely, and act so too; and take nothing ill where no ill is meant; nay, where it is, 'twill easily forgive, and forget too, upon small acknowledgements.

Friend are true twins in soul; they sympathise in everything.

One is not happy without the other, nor can either of them be miserable alone. As if they could change bodies, they take their turns in pain as well as in pleasure; relieving one another in their most adverse conditions."

WILLIAM PENN (1644-1718)

– ◆ –

A FRIEND IN NEED

"A real friend is one who walks in when the rest of the world walks out."

WALTER WINCHELL (1879-1972)

— ◆ —

"How many of us today can actually strip our insides bare and say to somebody, 'Look, I really need you'. We can say 'I love you' twenty-seven times a day, but it's not like saying 'Look, here I am, vomit and all, sick and frightened. Recognize my need and my humanity.'"

ROD STEIGER

— ◆ —

"The test of friendship is assistance in adversity, and that, too, unconditional assistance."

MAHATMA GANDHI (1869-1948)

— ◆ —

Love is blind; friendship closes its eyes.

PROVERB

– ◆ –

"The proper office of a friend is to side with
you when you are in the wrong.
Nearly anybody will side with you
when you are in the right."

MARK TWAIN (1835-1910)

– ◆ –

"Henry IV of France one day reproached
the Count d'Aubigné, that he still retained
his friendship for M. de la Trémouillé, who
was in disgrace, and banished from the court.
'Sire,' said d'Aubigné, 'M. de la Trémouillé
is sufficiently unfortunate; since he has lost
the favour of his master, I could not abandon
him in the time when he has the most need
of my friendship."

THE PERCY ANECDOTES

WITHOUT A WORD, WITHOUT A SIGN

"I love you not only for what you are, but for
what I am when I am with you.

"I love you not only for what you have
made of yourself, but for what you
are making of me.

"I love you because you have done more than
any creed could have done to make me good,
and more than any fate could have done to
make me happy.

"You have done it without a touch,
without a word, without a sign.

"You have done it by being yourself. Perhaps
that is what being a friend means, after all."

ANONYMOUS

— ◆ —

TOGETHER

"Friends do not live in harmony merely, as some say, but in melody."

HENRY DAVID THOREAU (1817-1862)

— ◆ —

"I want someone to laugh with me, someone to be grave with me, someone to please me and help my discrimination with his or her own remark, and at times, no doubt, to admire my acuteness and penetration."

ROBERT BURNS (1759-1796)

— ◆ —

"The best moments of a visit are those which again and again postpone its close."

JEAN PAUL RICHTER (1763-1825)

— ◆ —

MAKING LIFE WORTHWHILE

"Friendship is the only cement that will ever
hold the world together."

WOODROW WILSON (1856-1924)

— ♦ —

"Friendship is unnecessary, like philosophy,
like art. . . . It has no survival value; rather it
is one of those things that give value
to survival."

C. S. LEWIS (1898-1963)

— ♦ —

"The bird a nest, the spider a web, man
friendship."

WILLIAM BLAKE (1757-1827)

— ♦ —

"Friendship's the wine of life."

EDWARD YOUNG (1683-1765)